just FELINE
FRIENDS

Published by Willow Creek Press
P.O. Box 147, Minocqua, Wisconsin 54548

Library of Congress Cataloging-in-Publication Data

Kuchler, Bonnie Louise, 1958-
 Just feline friends : a cat's tribute to comrades, companions & confidants /
compiled by Bonnie Louise Kuchler.
        p. cm.
 ISBN 1-59543-055-5 (hardcover : alk. paper)
 1. Cats--Pictorial works. 2. Photography of cats. 3. Quotations, English. I.
Title.
 SF446.K78 2004
 636.8'0022'2--dc22

2004009886

Printed in Canada

just FELINE FRIENDS

A Cat's Tribute to Comrades,
Companions & Confidants

DEDICATION
For Leslee, cat lover, writing-buddy, and friend

ACKNOWLEDGEMENTS

If I could blow a warm breeze from the balmy beaches
of Hawaii to the frosty north woods of Wisconsin,
I would. But a simple "thank you" to two incredible
people — publisher Tom Petrie and
editor Andrea Donner — will have to do.

And I must acknowledge Pumpernickel, Butterscotch,
Tiger, Frisky, Lady Priscilla, and Sir Poopalot,
who each contributed a lifetime of love.

γou meet your friend, your face brightens —
you have struck gold.

~Kassia (810-before 867)
Byzantine Abbess, poet, hymnographer

$\mathcal{W}$hat a thing friendship is, world without end!
How it gives the heart and soul a stir-up!

~Robert Browning (1812-1889)
English poet

$\mathcal{W}$e cannot tell the precise moment
when friendship formed.
As in filling a vessel drop by drop,
there is at last a drop which makes it run over;
so in a series of kindnesses there is at last
one which makes the heart run over.

~Dr. Samuel Johnson (1709-1784)
English author and lexicographer

$\mathcal{F}$riendships are glued together with little kindnesses.

~Mercia Tweedale (b. 1915)

A true friend is someone who is there for you
when he'd rather be anywhere else.

~Len Wein
American author

$\mathcal{W}$ishing to be friends is quick work,
but friendship is a slow-ripening fruit.

~Aristotle (384-322 B.C.E.)
Greek philosopher, student of Plato, tutor of Alexander the Great

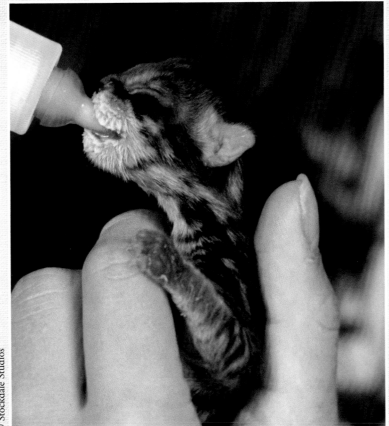

$\mathcal{F}$riendship… can run like a river,
quietly and sustainingly through life;
it can be an intermittent, sometime thing;
or it can explode like a meteor,
altering the atmosphere so that nothing
ever feels or looks the same again.

~Mary Haskell (1873-1964)
American writer and film critic

*A*nything, everything, little or big,
becomes an adventure
when the right person shares it.

~Kathleen Norris
American author

*S*hared joys make a friend.

~Friedrich Wilhelm Nietzsche (1844-1900)
German philosopher

$\mathcal{I}$ hold that companionship is a matter of mutual weaknesses. We like that man or woman best who has the same faults we have.

~George Jean Nathan (1882-1958)
American author, editor and drama critic

$\mathcal{F}$riends do not live in harmony merely,
as some say, but in melody.

~Henry David Thoreau (1817-1862)
American philosopher, author and naturalist

$\mathcal{F}$riendship is the sweetest form of love.

~Annie Gottlieb
American author

$\mathcal{W}$ith true friends, even water
drunk together is sweet enough.

~Chinese Proverb

No people feel closer or more friendly than those who are on the same diet.

~Unknown author

$\mathcal{F}$riendship is the bread of the heart.

~Mary Russell Mitford (1787-1855)
English dramatist, poet and essayist

$\mathcal{L}$et's face it, friends make life a lot more fun.

~Charles R. Swindoll
American minister and author

$\mathcal{T}$hat is what you love a friend for:
the ability to change your vision, bring back
your best self when you feel worst,
remind you of your strengths when you feel weak.

~Erica Jong
American author

A real friend helps us think our best thoughts,
do our noblest deeds, be our finest selves.

~Unknown author

$\mathcal{A}$ loyal friend laughs at your jokes when they're not so good, and sympathizes with your problems when they're not so bad.

~Arnold H. Glasgow
American psychologist

A friend is, as it were, a second self.

~Cicero

$\mathcal{T}$here is no greater loan than a sympathetic ear.

~Frank Tyger
American author

$\mathcal{B}$eing a friend means mastering the art of timing.
There is a time for silence. A time to let go and allow
people to hurl themselves into their own history.
And a time to pick up the pieces when it's all over.

~Gloria Naylor (b. 1950)
American writer

Silences make the real conversations between
friends. Not the saying but the never
needing to say is what counts.

~Margaret Lee Runbeck
American author

*T*he friend who can be silent with us in a
moment of despair or confusion, who can stay
with us in an hour of grief and bereavement,
who can tolerate not knowing, not curing,
not healing and face with us the reality of our
powerlessness, that is a friend who cares.

~Henri J. M. Nouwen (1932-1996)
Dutch-American author and priest

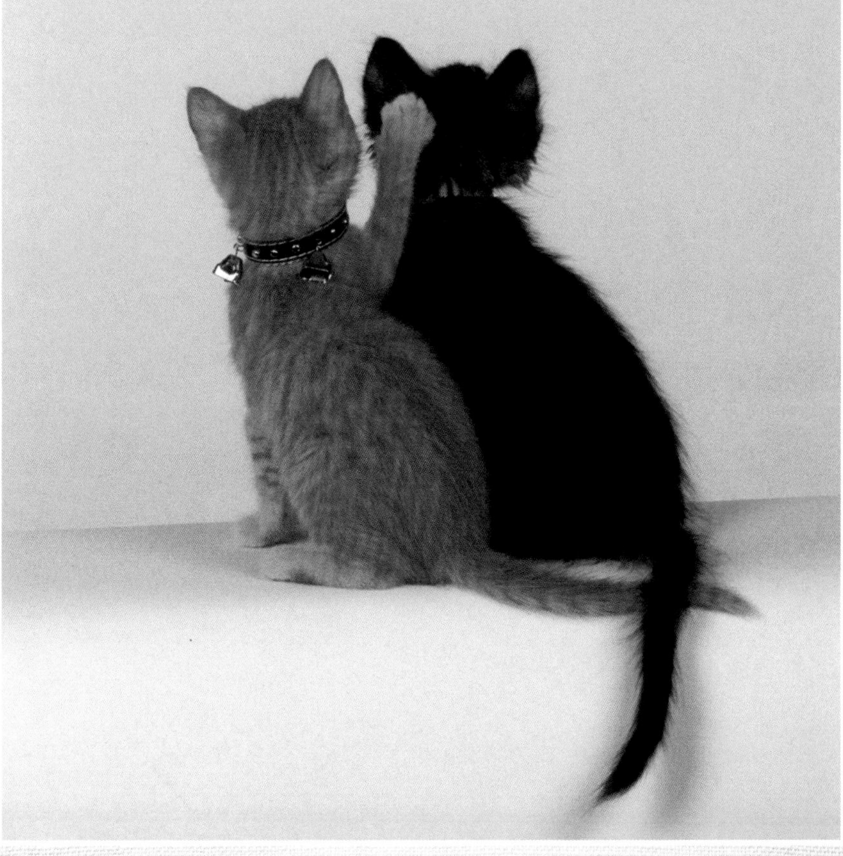

$\mathcal{W}$alking with a friend in the dark
is better than walking alone in the light.

~Helen Keller (1880-1968)
American deaf-blind author and lecturer

Nothing in this world appeases loneliness as does a flock of friends! There is always at least one who will understand, inspire, and give you the lift you may need at the time.

~George Matthew Adams
American author

$\mathcal{D}$o not protect yourself with a fence,
but rather by your friends.

~Czechoslovakian proverb

$\mathcal{T}$rouble is a great sieve
through which we sift our acquaintances;
those who are too big to pass through are friends.

~Arlene Francis (1907-2001)
American actress

*W*hat a great blessing is a friend, with a heart
so trusty you may safely bury all your secrets in it.

~Seneca (c. 3 B.C. - A.D. 65)
Roman philosopher, dramatist and statesman

$\mathcal{F}$ew delights can equal the mere presence
of one whom we trust utterly.

~George MacDonald (1824-1905)
Scottish novelist and poet

$\mathcal{T}$he greatest sweetener of human life is Friendship.

~Joseph Addison (1672-1719)
English essayist

$\mathcal{T}$he supreme happiness of life is the conviction
of being loved for yourself, or more correctly,
being loved in spite of yourself.

~Victor Hugo (1802-1885)
French poet and novelist

$\mathcal{I}$t is difficult to say who does you the most mischief:
enemies with the worst intentions,
or friends with the best.

~Edward George Bulwer-Lytton (1803-1873)
English novelist and politician

$\mathcal{D}$o not use a hatchet to remove
a fly from your friend's forehead.

~Chinese proverb

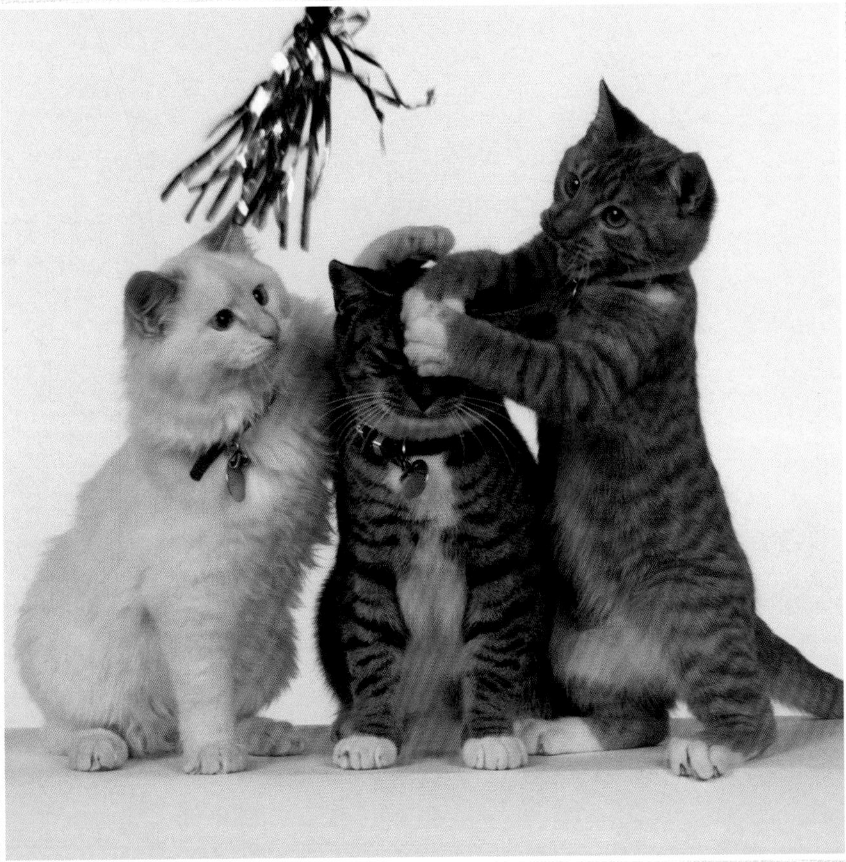

*F*unny, you don't look like a friend.
Ah, but they never do.

~Grace Metalious (1924-1964)
American author

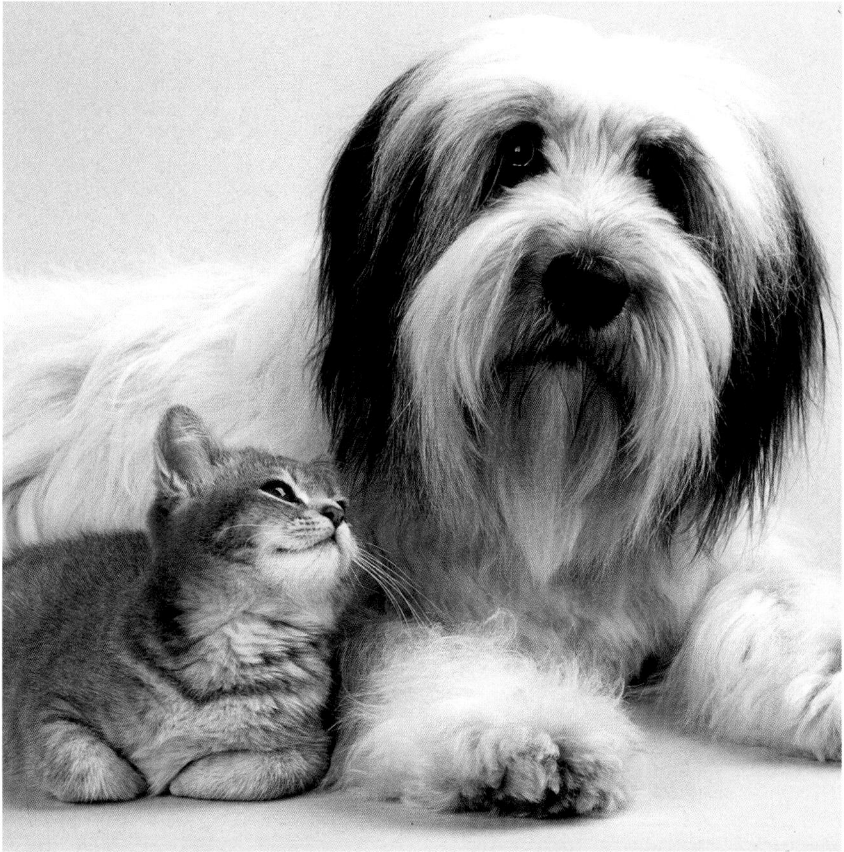

*W*hat do we live for, if it is not to make life less difficult for each other?

~George Eliot (1819-1880)
(pseudonym of Mary Ann Evans Cross)
English novelist and poet

© Bonnie Nance

$\mathcal{F}$riendship that flows from the heart
cannot be frozen by adversity,
as the water that flows from the spring
cannot congeal in winter.

~James Fenimore Cooper (1789-1859)
American author

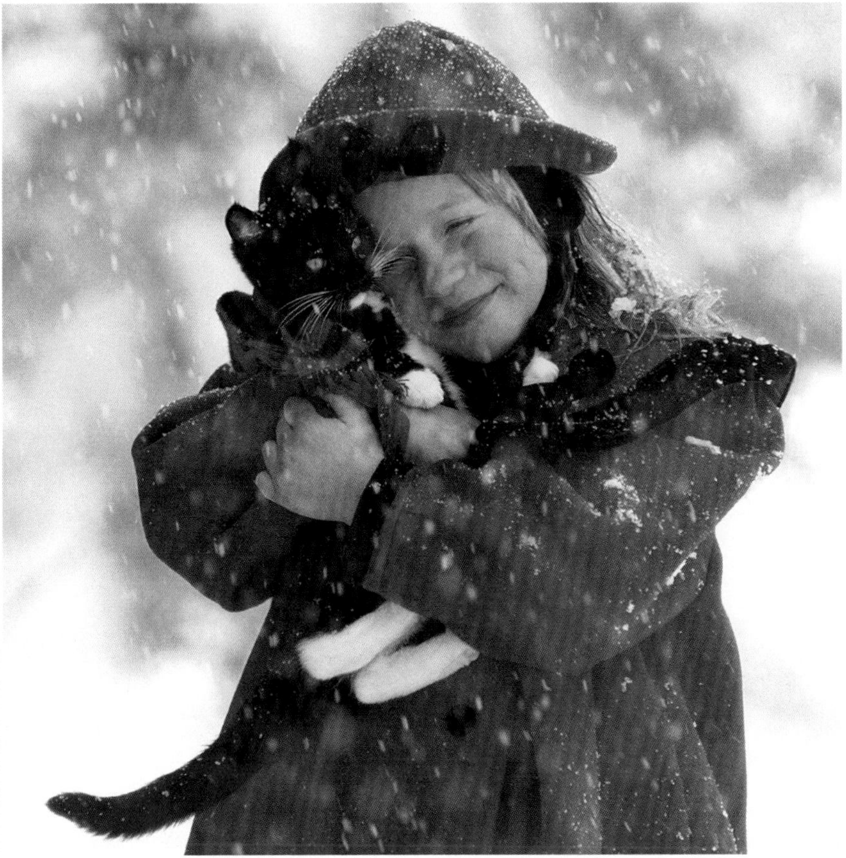

*F*riendship is a word, the very sight of which in print makes the heart warm.

~Augustine Birrell (1850-1933)
English politician, author and critic

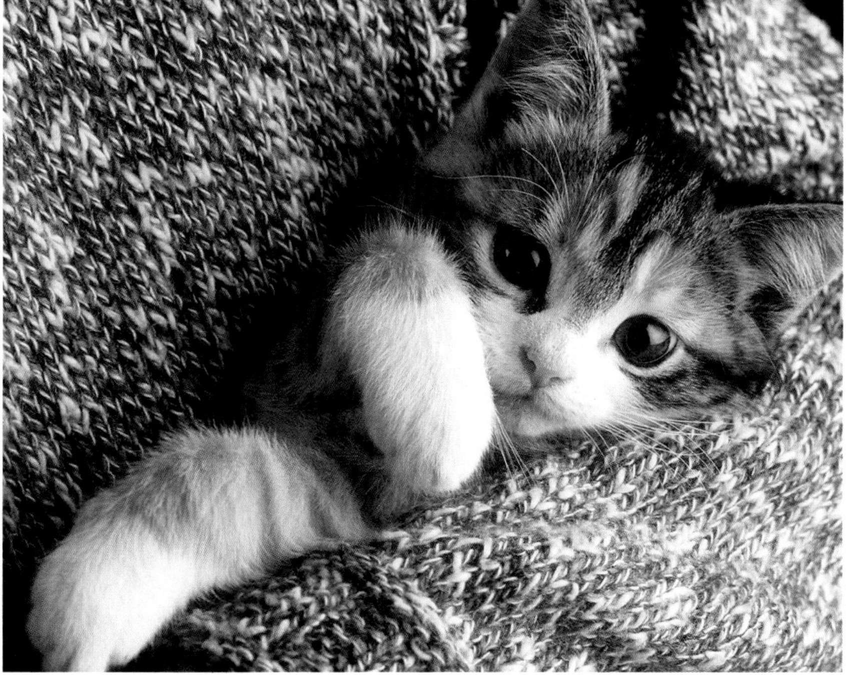

*I*ndeed, we do not really live unless we have friends surrounding us like a firm wall against the winds of the world.

~Charles Hanson Towne (1877-1949)
American editor and poet

A good friend is an umbrella for the heart.

~Unknown author

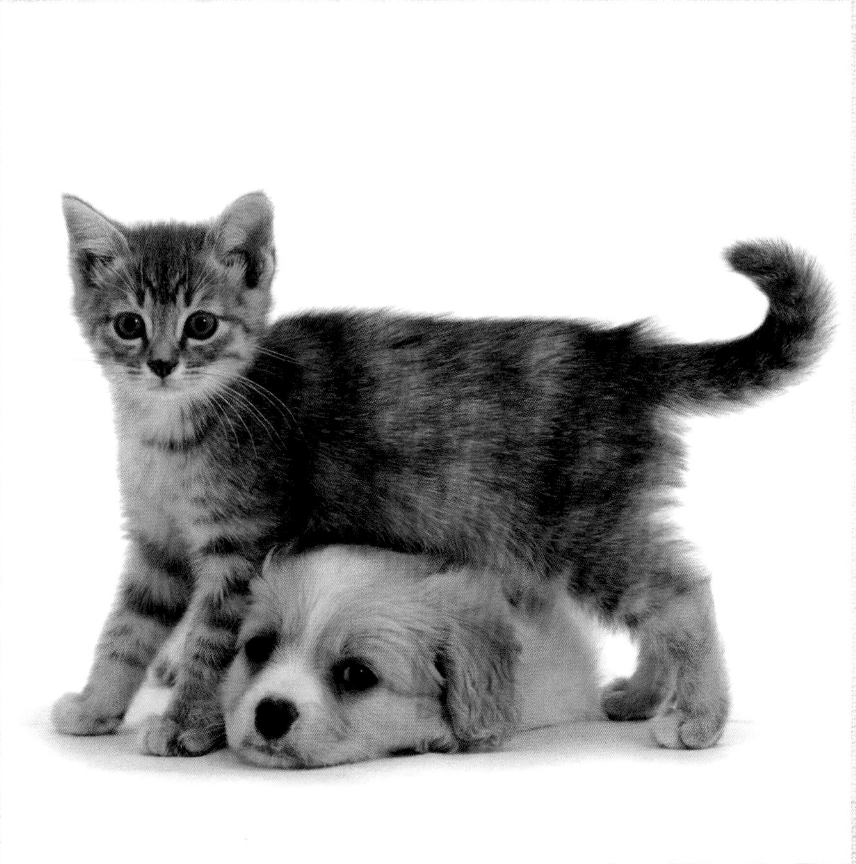

$\mathcal{F}$riendship is unnecessary, like philosophy, like art…
It has no survival value; rather it is one of those
things that give value to survival.

~C.S. (Clive Staples) Lewis (1898-1963)
English literary scholar and author

*W*hat brings joy to the heart is not so much the friend's gift as the friend's love.

~Saint Aelred of Rievaulx (1100-1167)
English abbot, homilist and historian

*F*riendship is the golden thread
that ties the heart of all the world.

~John Evelyn (1620-1706)
English writer and gardener

$\mathcal{F}$riends are like windows through which you see out into the world and back into yourself.

~Merle Shain
American author

$\mathcal{W}$herever you are it is your own
friends who make your world.

~William James (1842-1910)
American philosopher, psychologist and writer

$\mathcal{N}$othing makes the earth seem so spacious
as to have friends at a distance…

~Henry David Thoreau (1817-1862)
American philosopher, author and naturalist

A friend is someone who allows
you distance but is never far away.

~Noah benShea
Canadian-American philosopher, poet and author

$\mathscr{A}$ constant friend is a thing rare and hard to find.

~Plutarch (c. 46 - 120)
Greek philosopher and biographer

$\mathcal{I}$ keep my friends as misers do their treasure, because, of all the things granted us by wisdom, none is greater or better than friendship.

~Pietro Aretino (1492-1556)
Italian satirist

© Randy Handwerger

*H*old a true friend with both your hands.

~Kanuri proverb, Nigeria

$\mathcal{M}$any people will walk in and out
of your life, but only true friends
will leave footprints in your heart.

~Eleanor Roosevelt (1884-1962) (attributed)
American humanitarian and diplomat

Bibliography

Grateful acknowledgement is made to the authors and publishers for use of the following material. If notified, the publisher will be pleased to rectify an omission in future editions.

Andrews, Robert, ed. *The Columbia Dictionary of Quotations*. New York: Columbia University Press, 1993.

Baker, Brian. (2001) "QuoteWorld.org – Over 15,000 Quotations and Famous Quotes," http://www.quoteworld.org. [accessed 24 February 2004]

Booher, Dianna. *Fresh-cut Flowers for a Friend*. Nashville: J. Countryman, a division of Thomas Nelson, Inc., 2002.

Bresnick, Peggy, ed. *Friends Forever: A Book of Quotations*. Kansas City: Andrews McMeel Publishing, 1997.

Copan, Lil, comp. *The Fabric of Friendship*. Wheaton, IL: Harold Shaw Publishers, 1996.

Craik, Dinah Maria Mulock. *A Life for a Life*. London: Hurst and Blackett, 1859.

DeFord, Deborah, ed. *Reader's Digest Quotable Quotes*. Pleasantville, New York: The Reader's Digest Association, Inc., 1997.

Dundon, Kaitlin, comp. (2001) One Heart Studio, "Book of Quotes" http://www.oneheartstudio.com [accessed 28 February 2004].

Engelbreit, Mary *Words For Friends To Live By*. Kansas City: Andrews McMeel, 2001.

Freeman, Dr. Criswell, comp. and ed. *Friends are Forever*. Nashville: Walnut Grove Press, 1998.

Goodman, Ted, ed. *The Forbes Book of Business Quotations: Thoughts on the Business of Life*. New York: Black Dog & Leventhal Publishers, 1997.

Hayes, Cyndi. *Book of Friendship: Making Life Better*. Kansas City: Andrews McMeel, 2001.

Klein, Allen. *Lift-Your-Spirits Quote Book*. New York: Gramercy (an imprint of Random House Value Publishing), 2001.

Klein, Allen. *Up Words for Down Days*. New York: Gramercy Books (an imprint of Random House), 1998.

Mead, Lucy, comp. *Friends are Special: A Tribute to Those Who Accept, Support & Care.* New York: Gramercy Books (an imprint of Random House Value Publishing), 2001.

Mjolsness, Jane, illus. *Friends: A Treasury of Quotations.* Philadelphia: Running Press, 1998.

Nouwen, Henri J. M. *Out of Solitude: Three Meditations on the Christian Life.* Notre Dame, IN: Ave Maria Press, 1984.

Phillips, Bob. *Phillip's Book of Great Thoughts & Funny Sayings.* Wheaton, IL: Tyndale House Publishers, 1993.

Roosevelt, David B. *Grandmere: A Personal History of Eleanor Roosevelt.* New York: Warner Books, 2002.

Thoreau, Henry David. *A Week on the Concord and Merrimack Rivers, "Wednesday."* London: Walter Scott, 1889.